KU-185-349

Staffordshire Library and Information Services
Please return or renew by the last date shown

If not required by other readers, this item ma
renewed in person, by post or telephone, o
email. To renew, either the book or ticket

24 Hour Renewal Line
0345 33 00 740

81063/16

SCHOOLS LIBRARY SERVICE

3 8023 00656 8073

Words I Use

Around the Town

Victoria Huseby

FRANKLIN WATTS
LONDON·SYDNEY

First published in 2005 by
Franklin Watts
96 Leonard Street
London
EC2A 4XD

Franklin Watts Australia
45–51 Huntley Street
Alexandria, NSW 2015

© Franklin Watts 2005

Editor: Rachel Tonkin
Series design: Mo Choy
Art director: Jonathan Hair
Photographer: Chris Fairclough
Literacy consultant: Gill Matthews

The Publishers would like to thank Post Office Ltd 2005
for the photograph reproduced on pages 8-9.

A CIP catalogue record for this book
is available from the British Library

ISBN: 0 7496 6085 6

Dewey classification: 307.76

Printed in China

STAFFORDSHIRE
SCHOOLS LIBRARY SERVICE

3 8023 00656 80173	
GEMMA	307. 76
JULY 05	£11.99

Contents

About this book
This book helps children to learn key words in the context of when and where they are used. Each picture is described in the main text, and the words in bold are labelled on the picture along with other key words, as a starting point for discussion. The open-ended questions will also help with language development. On pages 22-23 a simple quiz encourages children to look again in detail at all the pictures in the book, and this can be used to develop referencing skills.

street lights

traffic

shop

bus

traffic lights

4

road

pavement

Around the town

Towns are busy places. The streets are lined with **shops**. **Buses** and cars drive on the **road**. People walk safely on the **pavement**, away from the **traffic**.

?

Street lights help us to see in the dark. What other things in the picture help us to keep safe?

5

market stall

plantains

avocado pears

spinach

At the market

Towns often have markets with lots of different stalls. You can buy fruit and vegetables, like **melons**, **cucumbers** and **peppers**, from this **market stall**.

peppers

mushrooms

cucumbers

mangoes

melons

oranges

What other fruit and vegetables can you buy at this stall?

In the post office

In the post office, you can buy stamps, pay bills, and send letters and parcels. There are **weighing scales** on the **counter** so you can find out how much it will cost to send your post.

?

What other things can you do in a post office?

glass partition

counter

clock

leaflets

post office clerk

weighing scales

chair

waiter

table

cup

glass

saucer

menu

At the café

In town, people often meet their friends in a café. You choose what you want to eat and drink from a **menu**. The **waiter** brings your order to the **table**.

What different things can you see on the tables of this café?

pavement

zebra crossing

bollard

Crossing the road

A **zebra crossing** helps you to cross
the **road** safely. You have to wait on the
pavement until the **cars** stop for you.

billboard

clock

platform number

people

luggage

At the railway station

Railway stations are very busy places. **People** check the **clock** to see whether it's time to catch their train. The **platform number** tells them where to go.

What different things are people doing in this station?

toilets

ticket machine

Going to the library

In the **library** in the town you can borrow **books**, and also other things like maps, CDs, videos or DVDs. This library is in an old building. It has a big **door** and lots of **windows**.

library

opening times

door

book

? You can get to this library by bus. What other ways could you get there?

BUS STOP

Teddington Library

towards
Fulwell

33

bus stop

window

bike stand

17

At the supermarket

At the supermarket, you push a **trolley** up and down the **aisles**. You pick the things you want to buy off the **shelves** and put them in your trolley.

weighing scales

pineapples

bananas

BANANAS 39p

BANANAS 39p

BANANAS 39p

shelves

?

What different fruits are for sale in this supermarket?

sign

bag

aisle

trolley

19

Waiting for the bus

There are lots of **buses** in town, going to different places. People can find out what time their bus goes by looking at the **timetable**. They wait at the **bus stop** until the right bus comes.

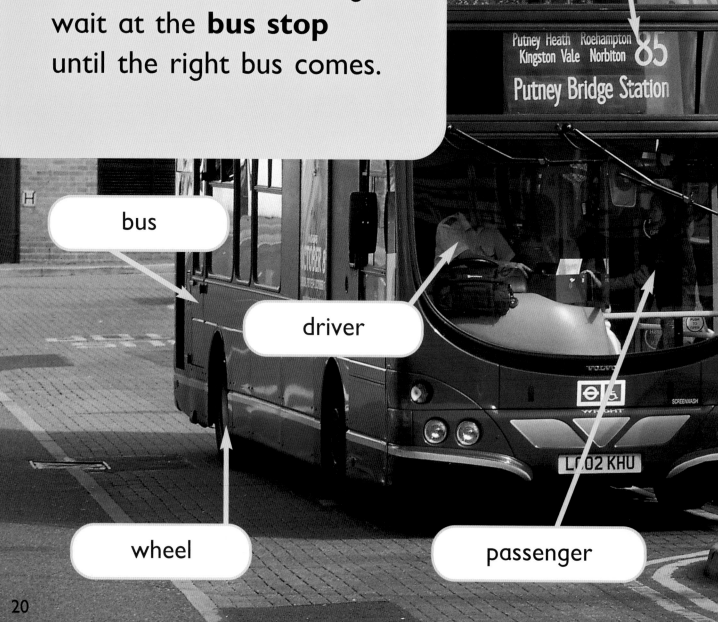

bus number

Putney Heath Roehampton
Kingston Vale Norbiton 85

Putney Bridge Station

bus

driver

wheel

passenger

LC02 KHU

Can you spot...?

Bunches of bananas.

The front of a bus.

Fruit on a market stall.

Melons for sale.

A menu.

A post office clerk.

Scales for weighing post.

A stand for a bike.

A table in a café.

A ticket machine.

Traffic lights.

A zebra crossing beacon.

Index